Nuclear War

Survival Skills and Prepping

Macallister Anderson

Copyrights

All rights reserved © Anderson Macallister and Maplewood Publishing. No part of this publication or the information in it may be quoted from or reproduced in any form by means such as printing, scanning, photocopying, or otherwise without prior written permission of the copyright holder.

Disclaimer and Terms of Use

Effort has been made to ensure that the information in this book is accurate and complete. However, the author and the publisher do not warrant the accuracy of the information, text, and graphics contained within the book due to the rapidly changing nature of science, research, known and unknown facts, and internet. The author and the publisher do not hold any responsibility for errors, omissions, results using the information in this book or contrary interpretation of the subject matter herein. Consider all information in this book to be for entertainment purposes and not professional advice, and to be used at your own risk. The author and publisher of this book cannot be held responsible for the consequences of your actions and it is understood that you will use the information in accordance to the laws of your own country. This book is presented solely for motivational, entertainment and informational purposes only.

ISBN: 978-1548986896

Printed in the United States

Contents

Introduction 1
History of Warfare 3
Different Methods of Warfare and Survival Techniques 5
Nuclear Weapons 7
    Countries That Currently Have Nuclear Weapons 8
    Effects of Nuclear Weapons on Human Health 8
Nuclear War 11
    History of Nuclear War 13
    Current Conflicts Involving Countries with Nuclear Weapons 20
Preparing to Survive Nuclear War 23
    Shelter 24
    Cooling and Ventilation of Shelters 27
    Carbon Monoxide and Fire Protection 30
    Food 32
    Water 34
    Meters for Radioactive Fallout 38
    Light 39
    Shelter Sanitation and Preventive Medicine 40
    Self-Treatment and Medication 41
    Shelter Furnishings 42
    Protective and Clothing Items 42
    Protection 43
    When War Is Imminent 43
    Things to Do Prior to an Attack 44
    During the Attack 45
    Minimum Pre-Crisis Preparation 47
Conclusion 51
Further Reading 53
Also by Macallister Anderson 55

Introduction

Since the beginning of the world, conflict between individuals and groups has occurred as a result of various issues. It stems mostly from disagreement on a particular issue on which neither party wants to budge. In some of these cases, the disagreement degenerates into conflict. Conflict is referred to as war when it involves a group of individuals, usually a society or nation state, and the use of arms or other deadly force. Wars often result in many casualties as lives and property are destroyed on a large scale, depending on the resolve and military sophistication of the parties involved.

The victims of war often include those who were not responsible for the war and those who are not directly involved. Usually warring societies will send soldiers, who could be trained or untrained, to the front lines. These soldiers will be equipped for the war, although perhaps not properly equipped due to logistical issues. However, anybody who is present in the area where the war is fought could become a victim. Individuals who are not directly involved in the war may be able to save themselves by taking certain precautions. Taking the right precautions can significantly boost an individual's chances of surviving the war. Many different types of weapons have been used over time, and as technology has improved, the lethality of such weapons has naturally increased. A variety of equipment has been developed to help soldiers and individuals protect themselves during a war.

Apart from the many state-to-state conflicts that have occurred, there have also been larger wars in which a number of countries form an alliance to fight against another country or group of countries. A major characteristic of any armed conflict or war is the destruction of life and property. Countries attempt to protect their civilian populations, both by maintaining a strong military and by establishing internally displaced person (IDP) camps to which refugees can relocate under the care of the government. Personal preparation is, however, just as important, if not more important, towards surviving a war. Knowing what to do and being prepared beforehand is a very important way of giving yourself a better chance. The first thing that you will need is information on what to expect and how to prepare. This information will guide your actions. The purpose of this book is specifically to provide all the information you will need about preparing to survive a nuclear war.

History of Warfare

The Mesolithic Cemetery site provides the oldest archeological evidence of war. It is believed this war happened about 14,000 years ago. Signs of violent death are observed on more than 40 percent of the skeletons in the cemetery. The incidence of war increased about 5,000 years ago with the rise of nation states. This resulted in increased military activity, technological advances and eventually the invention of gunpowder. Spears, swords and arrows gave way to more deadly guns and bombs. It is believed that between 3,500 BC and the end of the 20th century, about 14,500 wars have been fought. It is also estimated that about 3.5 billion people have died as a result of these wars. This includes direct casualties as well as people who died from war-related diseases or starvation.

Only about 15 percent of these deaths are believed to have occurred during the primitive era. During this era, almost all societies – upwards of 90 percent – engaged in frequent wars. However, these wars were not organized and the combatants did not get any formal military training.

The remaining 85 percent of war deaths occurred after the primitive era. During this era, steady improvements in technology also led to a steady advancement in weaponry. The result was that wars became more deadly. While most of these wars were between countries, many others were between different factions within a country, such as when one ethnic or social group fought another. Here are some recent wars listed in ascending order of casualties:

- The Russian Civil War and foreign intervention between 1917 and 1922 led to the death of 5 to 9 million people.
- The Dungan Revolt between 1862 and 1877 led to the death of 16 million people.

- The conquests of Tamerlane between 1370 and 1405 led to the death of 20 million people.
- The second Sino-Japanese war between 1937 and 1945 led to the death of 20 million people.
- The Qing Dynasty's conquest of the Ming Dynasty between 1616 and 1662 led to the death of 25 million people.
- The An Shi Rebellion between 755 and 763 led to the death of about 36 million people.
- World War I between 1914 and 1918 led to the death of 39 million people.
- The Taiping Rebellion between 1850 and 1864 led to the death of 40 million people.
- The Mongol conquests in the 13th century led to the death of 60 million people.
- World War II between 1939 and 1945 led to the death of between 60 and 85 million people.

Many of these wars went on for over 10 years. To survive a war of such length, people in the affected regions must have taken precautions, and that implies that they were able to get accurate information and act on it.

The development of peacemaking international organizations such as the United Nations has led to a considerable reduction in wars between countries. However, internal conflicts have continued to occur frequently. Furthermore, current tensions between certain nations have sparked fears that World War III could begin at any time. As some of these nations are current or aspiring nuclear powers, the potential for the use of nuclear weapons has made it important to inform people about preparations that might save their lives in the event of a nuclear attack.

Different Methods of Warfare and Survival Techniques

Many different methods have been used for waging warfare over the years. Many of these methods are still being used, and some may be used again: Albert Einstein famously remarked, "I know not with what weapons World War III will be fought, but World War IV will be fought with sticks and stones." Combatants usually wage war with all the resources at their disposal, and thus a nuclear attack would most probably be accompanied by more conventional forms of warfare. Knowing about survival techniques for conventional wars is therefore also important. Fortunately, most of the survival techniques are related. Much of what this book discusses about preparing to survive a nuclear war applies to other types of warfare as well.

In primitive times, the basic weapons of war were spears and swords. The fact that the soldiers had no formal training made it considerably easier to survive. There were no weapons of mass destruction, no missiles or artillery, nothing that required sophisticated defensive measures. All that was needed was a shield to defend oneself and a spear or sword to attack the enemy. Further, battlefields were generally located away from residential areas. Civilians, therefore, only had to hope that their own soldiers were successful; if so, they were unlikely to be in any danger. On the other hand, a victorious army would often overrun enemy villages and towns, killing, looting, raping and taking slaves. In other cases, they would simply establish their authority over the conquered territory.

With the invention of gunpowder and guns, it became much easier to kill people during war. Guns were lethal even at great distances until the invention of bulletproof vests. There are many different types of guns, some with more stopping power, some with a greater rate of fire. The invention of vehicles changed the platform for war again. Tanks, battleships and aircraft necessitated stronger weapons like rocket propelled grenades (RPGs) and high-explosive bombs.

There are a number of non-conventional weapons that have also been developed. Some of these weapons are very deadly and very much discouraged. These include biological and chemical weapons. Many countries have signed treaties against their use.

Biological warfare entails the use of biological toxins or infectious agents such as fungi, viruses and bacteria with the aim of incapacitating or killing plants, animals and humans. Entomological warfare (insect warfare) is also included in the definition of biological warfare. Chemical warfare, on the other hand, is when chemical substances with toxic properties are used as weapons. Biological and chemical warfare are just as dangerous as nuclear warfare, especially when used in a full-scale attack. Despite the treaties, there is also no assurance that such weapons will not be used if a nation possessing the capability sees it as the only chance of defeating an opponent. As with other types of warfare, the best defense is to stay away from areas at high risk of biological or chemical attack.

For virtually any type of warfare, the surest way to ensure survival is to move to an area where the threat of attack is low to zero. If no bombs are being dropped or bullets fired where you live, none will hit you, intentionally or otherwise. However, this is not always feasible, as nobody can predict locations which will be completely safe from war. The best chance is to opt for a place where there is currently no threat of war. It often happens that war breaks out suddenly, leaving little to no time to relocate. Even when there is some time, relocation is likely to be very difficult once hostilities have commenced. Everyone else will be trying to escape too, and roads, train stations and airports will be severely overcrowded. If possible, though, getting to a hidden, secure location stocked with enough water, food and other necessities can go a long way toward helping you survive.

Nuclear Weapons

A nuclear weapon can be defined as an explosive device whose destructive force results from nuclear fission (fission bomb) or from combining nuclear fusion and fission (thermonuclear weapon). Either method releases a huge amount of energy from a relatively small amount of matter. The first test of an atomic (fission) bomb gave the same quantity of energy as about 20,000 tons of TNT. A 1.2-ton thermonuclear weapon, on the other hand, can produce an explosion equivalent to 1.2 *million* tons of TNT. These bombs are so powerful that it is possible for a whole city to be devastated by a nuclear device that is the same size as a conventional bomb. This is achieved through radiation, fire and blast. Nuclear weapons are therefore classified as weapons of mass destruction. Ever since they were invented, efforts at the international level have attempted to control how these weapons are used.

The boosted fission bomb is another type of nuclear weapon. This type of bomb is able to increase the effect of its explosion with the assistance of subsidiary fusion reactions, but it is not a fusion bomb. The fusion reactions produce neutrons that primarily improve the efficiency of the fission. Boosted fission bombs are of two types: an externally boosted type where concentric shells of depleted uranium and lithium-deuteride are layered over the fission bomb's core; and an internally boosted type where a mixture of deuterium-tritium is injected into the core of the bomb.

The United States has used two nuclear weapons in war, both against Japan at the end of World War II. The United States Army Air Forces dropped two bombs on two different Japanese cities within three days. The first bomb, nicknamed Little Boy, was detonated over Hiroshima on 6 August 1945, while Fat Man was detonated over Nagasaki on 9 August. Both were fission bombs. About 200,000 military personnel and civilians died as a result of the explosions.

This was the only combat use of nuclear weapons to date, but it was followed by more than two thousand test detonations. The Treaty on the Non-Proliferation of Nuclear Weapons was developed with the aim of reducing the spread of these exceptionally powerful weapons. However, the effectiveness of the treaty has been threatened.

Countries That Currently Have Nuclear Weapons

Only a few countries are known to possess nuclear weapons. However, it is possible that a few more countries have nuclear weapons but do not acknowledge it. The US was the first country to test a nuclear weapon (in 1945), and is the only country to have used a nuclear bomb during war (also in 1945, against Japan). Russia also has nuclear weapons, having developed them in 1949 while still part of the Soviet Union. Other countries that have acquired nuclear weapons include the United Kingdom in 1952, France in 1960, the People's Republic of China in 1964, India in 1974, Pakistan in 1998, and North Korea in 2006. The Netherlands, Belgium, Turkey, Italy and Germany are nuclear weapons sharing states. It is believed that Israel possesses nuclear weapons, but the Jewish state pursues a deliberate policy of ambiguity under which it does not acknowledge this fact. South Africa developed nuclear weapons in the past, but has dismantled them and renounced its nuclear status.

Effects of Nuclear Weapons on Human Health

It has been estimated that the wartime detonation of about 100 Hiroshima-type atomic bombs would result in the deaths of tens of millions of people from the effects on the climate alone. The hypothesis is that each bomb would cause a firestorm, which would release a great deal of soot into the atmosphere. This could cover the earth, drastically reducing the amount of sunlight reaching the surface for years. This situation, known as nuclear winter, would result in massive food chain disruption.

The atomic bomb dropped on Hiroshima produced four stages of medical effects. From these effects it can be predicted that larger nuclear bombs combining fission and fusion reactions will result in thermal and blast effects so serious that there would be few if any survivors around the blast location. The stages are as follows:

- Initial Stage: The initial stage runs from the first to the ninth week after detonation. In Hiroshima, the highest number of deaths occurred during this stage. About 10 percent of the deaths were due to exposure to lethal radiation, while the remaining 90 percent were caused by blast effects and/or thermal injury.
- Intermediate Stage: The intermediate stage covers the tenth through twelfth weeks. Median lethal range ionizing radiation (LD50) is the major cause of deaths during this period.
- Late period: The late period comprises the thirteenth through twentieth weeks. Survivors begin to recover during this period.
- Delayed period: The delayed period includes everything after 20 weeks. Many complications from the healing of mechanical and thermal injuries may be expected during this period. Blood disorders, decreased fertility and infertility may occur among survivors exposed to radiation of between few hundred and a thousand millisieverts. Those exposed to a dose of ionizing radiation of between 50 and 100 millisieverts will face an approximately 25 percent greater chance of dying from cancer during their lifetimes. The strength of the dose received will also influence the rate at which survivors will get cancer. This effect will be experienced around five years after

exposure to radiation. Lesser issues will include effects on tissues and organs in the body, such as eye cataracts.

Individual exposure to fallout will vary depending on the location and type of shelter. Those who flee perpendicular to the wind direction or who simply stay in their houses (shelter in place) will be able to avoid serious exposure to the fallout plume, especially if they continue to shelter for several weeks after the nuclear detonation. Their overall radiation dose will vary, but will be relatively low. They will be much safer compared to people who continue to go about their normal lives (leaving the safety of the shelter regularly for work, school or shopping).

Iodine-131 is the fallout isotope most hazardous to humans. Staying inside a shelter until after this isotope has decayed to about a tenth of a percent of its initial quantity will go a long way towards keeping an individual safe from harm. This amount of decay is equivalent to ten half-lives, which is about 80 days. Staying indoors for this many days after a nuclear attack can almost completely eliminate the risk of radiation-related thyroid cancer.

Nuclear War

Nuclear warfare, sometimes referred to as thermonuclear warfare or atomic warfare, is a political strategy of using nuclear weapons to attack the enemy in a military conflict. Nuclear weapons can quickly destroy the enemy on the battlefield, but the radiological dimension of nuclear warfare has long-lasting aftereffects due to the fallout. A major exchange of nuclear weapons might result in a nuclear winter lasting decades, centuries, or possibly as much as a thousand years. Anti-nuclear activists in the 1980s warned that nuclear winter could cause the extinction of the human race through starvation.

However, the nuclear winter theory is dismissed by some analysts. These analysts state that, even during the Cold War, nuclear weapon stockpiles were not vast enough to have kept rural populations from surviving a nuclear holocaust.

After the Soviet Union collapsed in 1991 and the Cold War ended, the fear of a nuclear exchange between the two superpowers waned. Despite this, the proliferation of nuclear weapons means that there is still concern about localized nuclear conflicts as well as nuclear terrorism.

Nuclear warfare can be divided into two categories. Different types of nuclear weapons would presumably be used in the different categories, producing different effects.

Limited nuclear war, which can also be referred to as a nuclear exchange or attack, entails the small-scale use of nuclear weapons by two or more belligerents. Limited nuclear war would probably target major enemy infrastructure, either civilian or military. For instance, military facilities could be targeted to destroy the enemy's ability to take defensive measures or stage a counterattack, prior to the use of conventional forces to carry out an invasion.

Full-scale nuclear war would involve the use of a huge quantity of nuclear weapons to attack as much of the enemy country as possible. This implies attack on civilian, economic and military targets. The entire military, social and economic infrastructure of the target country could be obliterated in such an attack. There could also be a devastating effect on the biosphere of the earth.

Some Cold War strategists, including Henry Kissinger, believed in the possibility of full-scale nuclear war between two superpowers such as the Soviet Union and the US. Others fear that a limited nuclear war might worsen and progress into a full-scale nuclear war. Others still have referred to limited nuclear war as slow motion global nuclear holocaust. This group believes that any limited nuclear war would normalize the use of nuclear weapons and would soon be followed by others. Before long, the whole earth would become inhabitable, just as in a full-scale nuclear war. In their view, limited nuclear warfare would just take a little longer to make the planet uninhabitable.

Experts are unanimous, however, that nuclear war in any form would quickly lead to the loss of millions of lives. Even the most optimistic admit that a major exchange of nuclear weapons will result in many deaths within a few days. The pessimists believe that the human race could become completely extinct following a full-scale nuclear war. Even in a best-case scenario, they expect only a very small number of survivors in remote areas. Such survivors would have greatly reduced quality of life and life expectancy.

The horrific catastrophe that would accompany a global nuclear war would certainly lead to irreversible damage to the global climate and ecosystems, as well as most complex life. If the predictions of nuclear winter are correct, then a change in the global power balance would also follow. Countries like Brazil, Argentina, China, India, New Zealand and Australia would probably become the new world superpowers if the current superpowers engaged in a full-scale nuclear exchange.

A presentation at the 2006 annual meeting of the American Geophysical Union showed that a limited nuclear war at the regional level could lead to as many deaths as the whole of World War II. Significant climate change would persist for 10 years or more. The authors of the study foresaw about 50 atomic bombs being used in a regional conflict between two subtropical nations. If the 50 bombs were the size of the one used on Hiroshima, 15 kilotons, between 2.6 million and 16.7 million lives could be lost in each country. They also estimated that the war would release about five million tons of soot, resulting in the cooling of Eurasia and North America (including important grain-growing regions) by many degrees. As the cooling would continue for many years, this would be catastrophic for food production.

There is also the possibility of an accidental nuclear war caused by inadvertent triggering of nuclear weapons. This could result from misunderstandings, overreaction to military exercises or unannounced missile tests, accidental incursions by enemy warplanes, deliberate nuclear attacks by rogue military commanders, or malfunctioning targeting computers and/or early warning devices.

History of Nuclear War
In 1945, towards the end of World War II, the US carried out atomic attacks on the Japanese cities of Hiroshima and Nagasaki on 6 and 9 August respectively. These remain the only times nuclear weapons have been used in war, and it is worth discussing what led up to them.

Six months earlier, the US Twentieth Air Force under General Curtis LeMay had carried out low-level incendiary raids on Japanese cities. The worst of these was the Operation Meetinghouse raid on Tokyo. On the night of 9/10 March, around 300 Boeing B-29 Superfortress bombers dropped some 1,665 tons of explosives and incendiaries on Tokyo. The attack achieved its aim of setting Tokyo's wooden buildings alight, and the resulting fire created a tornado-like wind moving at over 100 miles per hour. About 100,000 people were killed and 267,000 buildings destroyed over an area of 16 square miles. Operation Meetinghouse was the deadliest bombing raid in the history of military aviation, and the only conventional attack deadlier than the nuclear raids on Hiroshima and Nagasaki. Similar attacks on scores of other Japanese cities had killed close to half a million people by August.

Earlier in the year, the 10-week Battle of Okinawa had resulted in a quarter of a million deaths, including about 150,000 civilians. The US had developed a plan, christened Operation Downfall, to attack the Japanese home islands. Based on casualties suffered at Okinawa and other island-hopping battles, US commanders estimated that anywhere from 50,000 to 500,000 American soldiers would be killed, with up to a million wounded. (The US Army actually procured 500,000 Purple Heart decorations, awarded for death or injury in combat, in anticipation of the campaign.) Considering that more than 400,000 US soldiers had already lost their lives in the Pacific and European theaters of World War II, President Harry Truman concluded that he did not want to pay the price of Operation Downfall.

On 26 July 1945, the US, China and the United Kingdom issued the Potsdam Declaration, which demanded Japan's unconditional surrender. The demand came with a warning that failure to comply would result in utter and prompt destruction. The government of Japan replied that it would not surrender, and President Truman made good the threat by dropping atomic bombs on Hiroshima and Nagasaki. When these bombs were deployed, they were the only two atomic bombs in existence, although a third was scheduled for completion in September.

On 6 August, Little Boy, a uranium-based fission weapon, was released over Hiroshima, producing a blast equivalent to 15 kilotons of TNT and destroying the headquarters of the Japanese

Second General Army and 5th Division along with some 50,000 other buildings. About 20,000 Korean slave laborers, 20,000 Japanese soldiers, and 30,000 civilians were killed.

Just three days later, on 9 August, Fat Man, a plutonium-based fission weapon, was detonated over Nagasaki. Yielding about 20 kilotons, this bomb destroyed 60 percent of Nagasaki and killed about 35,000 people. Only 150 of these were Japanese soldiers, but the dead also included around 28,000 Japanese munitions workers and 2,000 Korean slave laborers. Because the bomb hit Nagasaki's industrial zone, it succeeded in eliminating about 80 percent of the city's non-dock industrial production.

On 15 August, six days after the attack on Nagasaki, Japan surrendered. The signing of the instrument of surrender on 2 September marked the end of World War II. In part because of the atomic attacks on Hiroshima and Nagasaki, Japan later adopted the Three Non-Nuclear Principles that forbid it from creating nuclear weapons.

The status of nuclear weapons in military and international relations was not clear immediately following the end of World War II. The US assumed that its atomic bombs would offset the larger conventional forces of the Soviet Union and could be used to exact concessions from Soviet leader Joseph Stalin. However, the Soviet Union soon acquired its own nuclear capability through both espionage and scientific research. This put the two superpowers on a fairly equal footing: The US was not sure that its nuclear arsenal could stop the Soviets from taking over Europe, while the Soviets worried that they did not have enough atomic bombs to defeat the Americans in a full-scale nuclear war.

The US shifted control over future nuclear development from the military to the civilian Atomic Energy Commission (AEC). This was a recognition of the unique benefits and risks of nuclear weapons as opposed to other military weapons.

Shortly after World War II ended, the US created a strategic force of Convair B-36 Peacemaker bombers capable of delivering nuclear payloads to potential enemies directly from US bases. The Americans also deployed atomic bombs at locations around the world as the need and opportunity arose. Within several years, many in the US defense community believed that the US was so dominant as to be invincible to nuclear attack, since any other country would be afraid to engage in a nuclear war.

There were many proposals, including from the newly formed United Nations, to place all nuclear weapons under the control of international bodies. The aim of this was to ensure that they were not used and to discourage other nations from building their own nuclear weapons resulting in an arms race. However, the US could not be persuaded to agree with these proposals.

The Soviets carried out their first nuclear weapon test on 29 August 1949 at Semipalatinsk in Kazakhstan. US scientists had warned that the Soviet Union was going to create its own nuclear weapons, but American officials had not believed it would happen so soon. They did not know that the Soviet Union had spied on their nuclear program at Los Alamos, mostly in the person of Klaus Fuchs, a theoretical physicist. The first Soviet bomb was thus a direct replica of the Fat Man plutonium device dropped on Nagasaki. In the same year, the US drafted its first plan for nuclear war with the Soviet Union, codenamed Operation Dropshot.

More countries soon joined the atomic club. In 1952, the UK carried out a test of its own autonomous nuclear weapon. France and China followed in 1960 and 1964 respectively. Even though European nuclear arsenals were not as large as those of the Soviet Union and the US, they played a vital role in strategic planning during the Cold War. A top secret white paper put together for the British government by the Royal Air Force in 1959 detailed the capability of nuclear-armed RAF bombers to destroy military targets and key cities in the Soviet Union. It estimated that a full-scale attack would kill about 16 million Soviet citizens, half of them instantly.

Despite the newfound nuclear capability of Soviet Union, when the Cold War started, the advantage was still with the Americans. Their more sophisticated weapons and bombers meant that the US had the ability to bomb the Soviet Union while the Soviet Union would have found it very difficult to bomb the mainland US.

By 1960, the US had developed its first single integrated plan for nuclear operations. It included targeting options, target sets, and procedures for launching nuclear weapons. Versions of this plan were in use until 2003. Development of the US Missile Defense Alarm System also started in 1960. This alarm system consisted of 12 satellites that would provide limited early warning in the event of an intercontinental ballistic missile launch from Soviet territory. The alarm system was ready by 1964.

A worrisome and complex situation occurred in 1962 when the Soviet Union placed medium-range ballistic missiles in Cuba just 90 miles from the US. This was a reaction to the American placement of Jupiter missiles in Turkey. Tense negotiations led to the US dismantling its Turkish launch sites after the Soviet Union had removed its missiles from Cuba. Following the Cuban Missile Crisis, the Soviet Union embarked on a massive nuclear buildup.

By the end of the 1960s, each side had so many warheads and ICBMs that their nuclear capabilities were almost balanced. Both the Soviet Union and the US had the ability to destroy the other's infrastructure and kill most of its people. Game theorists referred to this situation as mutually assured destruction (MAD) or balance of power. They believed there could be no outright winner of a full-scale nuclear war between the two countries; at best, one side would achieve a pyrrhic victory after suffering so much loss of life and property that it would be almost equivalent to a defeat. American and Soviet leaders seemed to accept this view, as they confined their conflict to low-intensity proxy wars.

Before the 1960s ended, China had started its Underground Project 131 and other subterranean infrastructure designed to survive a nuclear attack after the Sino-Soviet Split.

A drawback of the MAD doctrine was the possibility of nuclear warfare breaking out accidentally. The early warning systems then in existence were very much prone to error. For instance, in 1979 alone there were 78 missile display conferences to examine detections that suggested a potential threat to North America. On 26 September 1983, Soviet missile defense officer Stanislav Petrov received a convincing indication from the early warning system he was monitoring that the US had launched a first strike against the Soviet Union. Fortunately Petrov was able to identify it as a false alarm; he was later honored by the UN for his actions in avoiding a nuclear war. Bureaucratic failures, test programs, misidentification of migratory geese, and failed computer chips led to many other such incidents.

During the Cold War, the US Air Force kept nuclear-armed strategic bombers airborne every second of the day. Crews were rotated daily. The program was eventually scrapped due to a number of severe accidents, such as the 1968 Thule Air Base B-52 crash.

As a reaction to the 6 October 1973 Arab attack that started the Yom Kippur War, Israel built 13 nuclear weapons in a tunnel under the Negev desert. The weapons were subsequently distributed to units of the Israeli Air Force upon authorization by Minister of Defense Moshe Dayan, who further approved the use of the weapons to prevent Israel from being overrun.

India conducted her first nuclear test on 19 May 1974 at the Pokhran Test Range. The test, codenamed Smiling Buddha, was termed a "peaceful" nuclear explosion.

The Soviet Duga-3 over-the-horizon early warning radar system became operational in 1976. The very strong radio transmissions it used led to widespread disruption of civilian shortwave radio and earned it the nickname the Russian Woodpecker.

At the start of the 1980s, newly elected President Ronald Reagan was very committed to increasing the strength of the US military. In line with this, nuclear and conventional weapons programs received bountiful funding, and defensive systems were also developed.

The Cold War ended with the disintegration of the Soviet Union. Tensions between the US and Russia eased significantly, but the two countries retained huge arsenals of nuclear warheads and thus continued their nuclear standoff to some extent.

The September 11 attacks on the US saw the readiness level of US forces increased to the highest level in 28 years. While in the past Russia had increased its own readiness level whenever the US readiness level increased, in this instance the Russians actually curtailed their large-scale Arctic military exercises so as to reduce the incident risks.

A former chairman of the UN Disarmament Commission states that countries with known nuclear capabilities currently have over 16,000 tactical and strategic nuclear weapons ready to be deployed as well as 14,000 in storage. This does not include other countries which may have or be developing nuclear weapons. Israel is known to have deployable nuclear weapons. North Korea is believed they have up to 10. Pakistan has between 100 and 110; India has between 80 and 100. France has about 350 nuclear weapons, Britain has about 200, and China has about 400. Russia has about 8,500 nuclear weapons available for use and another 11,000 warehoused devices, while the US has about 7,000 ready for deployment and about 3,000 stored away. Countries with nuclear weapons see them as defensive weapons that deter attack. The theory is that a potential attacker would risk nuclear retaliation and the consequences of nuclear war.

Current Conflicts Involving Countries with Nuclear Weapons

Although the international community has been working very hard to prevent the use of nuclear weapons, there are some ongoing disputes that have the potential to result in nuclear warfare if not resolved peacefully.

One of these is between India and Pakistan. Neither state has ever signed the Non-Proliferation Treaty. It is believed that Pakistan built nuclear weapons in response to the Indo-Pakistani War of 1971 and India's own nuclear program. The brief Kargil War of 1999 occurred after the two countries already had nuclear weapons, and it is thought that Pakistan nearly used a nuclear weapon against India during this conflict. Considering the unresolved issue of Kashmir, the risk of nuclear warfare between the countries remains high.

Some military analysts also worry that a conflict could arise between China and the US over Taiwan. Any Taiwanese move towards independence might involve all three countries in a war, possibly a nuclear one.

Israel has fought a series of wars with neighboring countries in the Middle East as well as several non-state actors. Considering Israel's small size and population, a future attack might threaten to overwhelm it before it had enough time to respond by conventional means. In such a scenario, the use of nuclear weapons would become very likely.

On 7 March 2013, North Korea threatened the US with a preemptive nuclear strike and warned that foreigners should stay away from South Korea on 9 April. On 12 April the North Koreans stated that they were going to attack Japan and indicated that nuclear war was inevitable.

Apart from these currently known conflicts, new conflicts may arise between countries with nuclear weapons at any point, possibly with very short notice. Nuclear terrorism by non-state actors that have somehow acquired nuclear weapons is also a concern. For example, a nuclear power with an unstable government might lose control of its nuclear weapons to terrorists who could use them to attack that country or other countries. Nuclear terrorism could also take the form of dispersal of radioactive materials through the use of conventional explosives – so-called dirty bombs. A dirty bomb would not produce the injurious blast effects of a nuclear explosion, nor nearly as much radiation, but would still cause serious disruption. It would also necessitate expensive decontamination procedures, and would probably lead to increased spending on security.

Preparing to Survive Nuclear War

To survive a nuclear war, it is extremely important to have made preparations beforehand. The quality of these preparations will go a long way toward determining your chances of survival in the event of a nuclear attack. You must know what you need, how to get or make it, and what to do with it. You must also know what to do if a nuclear attack occurs. How much you know, and how accurate that information is, is vital. This book aims to provide you with detailed, comprehensive information about wars generally, about nuclear warfare, and most particularly about how to prepare to survive a nuclear attack. It includes a Further Reading section with a list of other useful resources.

You will need to get a number of things prior to a nuclear attack, preferably well in advance to avoid being taken unawares. Considering that wars often last for years, and that even a single nuclear detonation in your area will prevent you from going outside until the level of radioactivity has decreased, you will need to secure very large quantities of some items. The best way to accomplish this is to regularly stock up on supplies, especially food and water. You might want to budget a specific amount, say 15 percent of your monthly income, for preparation expenses. Hopefully nuclear warfare is still a few years away and this will give you enough time and money to acquire everything you need.

The items you will need to get will be discussed next. After that, we will discuss what you will need to do before, during and after a nuclear attack, up to the point when you can safely resume your normal life. (Which at this point could be far from normal, but at least you will be able to spend some time outside your bunker!)

When reviewing the items listed below, remember that you will need an adequate supply to last you for a minimum of 14 days. If there was just one nuclear detonation and the war has ended, it should be safe to come out by then. The more of these items you have, however, the better your chances of survival, especially if there are multiple nuclear attacks in your area and you need to stay in your shelter for months.

Shelter

Shelter is the most important necessity for surviving a nuclear war. This is not just a place to stay, however; a number of other things are also necessary. The shelter must be adequately equipped so that you can stay there for several days. It should also have the ability to properly protect you from radioactive fallout, as well as fire and blasts. We will discuss stocking your shelter later; first, here is how to build a reliable shelter that should be able to protect you during a nuclear attack.

Your location during an attack is key to determining your vulnerability. If you are outside, you will have no protection, and the probability of dying from the blast or radiation is therefore very high. A house will provide very slight protection, but most houses are not strong enough to withstand a nuclear blast. A nearby detonation could destroy the house, and will certainly break the windows. The flying glass could injure people inside, and the empty window frames will represent an entry point for radioactive fallout. If you do find yourself in a house during a nuclear attack, head for a windowless room, as you will be a bit safer there.

If your house has a basement, this will provide fair protection from both the blast and radioactive fallout. However, extra fortification is necessary to achieve the best possible protection.

A underground cellar or basement can be converted into a perfect nuclear shelter. It is even better if your basement is lined with concrete, as this will help protect you from gases and soil poisoning. To begin the conversion, first empty the cellar completely. This will give you more space to work with as well as a better idea of what you are working on. Next, you should add more insulation. Ideally you should cover the floor and walls with a fresh concrete layer, but even boards will help in a pinch. The idea is to have a thicker layer to protect yourself from poisoned dirt and gases. It will also help keep your cellar warm.

You will be spending at least several days in the cellar, so you will need a place to sleep. You should therefore add bunks to the cellar, one for every member of the family. It is advisable to get a couple of extra bunks as well, in case you have guests or neighbors to accommodate when an attack comes.

Make the bunks up with duvets and sheets, not blankets, which are more likely to be eaten by moths. It's also a good idea to supply each bed with a space blanket in case any of the sheets do become unusable. Space blankets will also come in handy in the event of extremely cold temperatures, when a duvet and a few sheets might not provide adequate warmth.

The whole idea of a shelter is to put some level of protection between yourself and the radioactive fallout. Fortunately, there are several common materials that will give you a great deal of protection. The following materials at the specified thickness will shield you from 99 percent of radiation:

- Solid brick at 16 inches
- Hollow concrete blocks at 16 inches, when filled with sand or mortar
- Packed dirt at two feet, or loose dirt at three feet
- Steel at 5 inches
- Lead at 3 inches
- Water at 3 feet

It is therefore possible to use these materials to build a fallout shelter, preferably somewhere very close to your house. A well-built shelter will shield you from radiation; all you need to do is to get into the shelter as soon as there is a nuclear attack, or preferably before. You should stay in the shelter during the period that the radiation is very intense.

Do not build a shelter under a tree. First of all, this will be more time-consuming and expensive because you will have to dig through or around the roots. More importantly, radioactive fallout that settles on the tree's branches and leaves will be able to get into your shelter through the roots, exposing you to gamma rays. This will not happen if your shelter is below solid earth.

If you live in a likely target area, such as close to an international airport, an industrial facility or a military base, then you will need more than just a radiation shelter. You will need a shelter that will be able to withstand a nuclear blast as well as radioactive fallout. A simple wood-framed shelter, with a wooden roof covered with about 3 feet of dirt, will be your best bet. Such a structure can withstand fire and blast at a 65 psi overpressure range, and so a blast from nuclear attack should not affect it. An in-house shelter does not provide the same degree of protection, since the blast and fire from the nuclear detonation could cause the house to collapse onto the shelter.

Most target areas will also have public shelters built and maintained by the government. People who live close to one or happen to be around it when an attack occurs will be able to seek refuge inside. However, public shelters have a number of drawbacks. They are generally large places that can house over 1,000 individuals, but they are still likely to become overcrowded in the event of an attack. Ventilation may be inadequate if fans go off because electrical power has been knocked out in the attack. Diseases may spread rapidly if any contagious individuals enter the shelter. As most such shelters have little to no food stored inside, food and water will soon become an issue, especially in an overcrowded shelter.

You will thus get the best protection from an earth-covered expedient blast and fallout shelter built for family use and stocked with the items discussed below. If your house is not within the blast radius, then an in-house shelter in a fortified basement or cellar will also provide excellent protection. If you have not made any personal provision for shelter, public shelters will give you some level of protection, as will an unfortified basement or cellar. Your house alone will afford very little protection if it does not have a basement or cellar.

Cooling and Ventilation of Shelters

It is very important to make adequate provision for cooling and ventilation of your shelter. Insufficient forced ventilation in an occupied shelter will rapidly cause unpleasant heat and humidity, especially during warm weather. How quickly the room becomes uncomfortable will depend on the ambient temperature and the number of people inside, as living bodies produce both water vapor and heat. In the long term, conditions in an unventilated shelter could become extreme enough to cause death.

The air in an underground fallout shelter will normally feel cool, even in the summer – but only until the shelter is occupied. Without ventilation, the ceiling, walls and floor will absorb as much body heat they are capable of absorbing within a few days. They will then begin to radiate heat back into the air, and the shelter can become unbearably hot in just a few hours. The only way to avoid this is to remove the body heat via circulated air. It is therefore very important to make sure that the shelter is properly ventilated for every season and will remain cool enough for comfortable occupation in excess of several days. It is true that an occupied, unventilated shelter might not get extremely hot in wintertime. Nevertheless, it is still vital to provide ventilation, as you cannot be certain when an attack will come or how long you will need to remain inside.

A common technique for ventilating a shelter is the use of an air pump. It is easy enough to buy a good air pump and install it in your shelter, and you can even make a manually operated air pump on your own. A manually operated pump is recommended since you can use it even if there is no electricity. Battery powered air pumps are available, but not advisable. The battery may have drained by the time you need to use it, and even fresh batteries will not last longer than a few days. Your pump should be able to pump in 40 cubic feet per minute of outdoor air per person. (You may be able to get away with less if your shelter is covered by a minimum of two feet of earth; in this case the insulation will be sufficient that it might not get unbearably hot for the occupants.)

Air should be moved gently to avoid increasing its temperature. The use of a high-speed electric pump will raise the air temperature by about 3°F. Body heat will then heat the air further. Ensure that the air is properly distributed throughout the room. In a trench shelter, for instance, it will be best if the air flows in through one end and out the other. However, in larger shelters, including basements, a setup where the air moves in a path from the pump to the exit point would leave other areas uncooled. In this situation it would be best to use more than one air pump.

Another option for ventilation is the use of directional fanning. However, this is significantly more laborious than the use of manually powered air pump, and may quickly become tiresome. A fan with two handles will be easier to make and use than a fan with a single handle. Overall, ventilation is very important in terms of health and comfort.

Every occupant of the shelter should have enough water to drink, along with salt. When food salt is included, every individual should get 10 grams or 1 tablespoon of salt and 4 quarts of water every day in hot weather. Wearing loose, lightweight clothes will also aid in sweat evaporation for efficient cooling, as air movement will be better able to dry skin. This also helps to prevent skin infections and heat rashes, which is an important consideration since medicines may be in short supply during nuclear warfare.

In freezing temperatures, an underground shelter covered with damp earth will be able to absorb the occupants' body heat. However, ventilation is still very important. Exhaled breath can cause a dangerous carbon dioxide buildup in a confined space. Early warning signs include deeper breathing and headaches.

Smoking should be prohibited in shelters with inadequate ventilation. Carbon monoxide and other substances in cigarette smoke can cause headaches even at low levels, so it may be necessary to prohibit smoking even next to the exhaust port.

Headache, collapse or death could also arise due to carbon dioxide from kerosene lanterns or open fires. These may be used in above-ground shelters with plenty of natural ventilation (although they can still make a room unbearably hot on a still day), but cannot be recommended for underground shelters, even in cold weather. Aside from the polluting gases, the heat will make the air in the shelter lighter than the outside air. The light, warm air will then escape through the exhaust vent or chimney, and cold air from the surface will sink into the shelter.

Research has shown that fallout particles that enter a shelter through an unfiltered ventilation system actually pose less risk than leaving the shelter unventilated. Thus, for small, family-type shelters, it is not essential to use air filters. The most dangerous fallout particles fall to the ground within hours of a nuclear explosion. Usually these particles are too large and falling too fast to be sucked into low-velocity air intake openings. Furthermore, only extremely small fallout particles are able to get into the lungs; the nose and bronchial passages filter out most particles bigger than 10 microns. In the hours after an attack, covering your nose and mouth with a cloth or dust mask can help to reduce the amount of big, hot fallout particles you are inhaling. This in turn reduces the risk of beta burns in the bronchial tubes, sinuses and nose.

Carbon Monoxide and Fire Protection

Carbon monoxide and fire are two often overlooked but vital dangers of nuclear warfare. In fact, they have been ranked as the third greatest safety issue in a nuclear attack, following blast effects and radioactive fallout. Generally, firestorms will only be a concern in cities where houses are built very close together. For suburban areas, the risk of a firestorm is minimal.

The bombing of Hiroshima produced a very serious firestorm that destroyed every building within a 4.4-square-mile area. This grew from several fires that started at almost the same time. Some of these were a direct result of the heat radiation from the atomic fireball, but many were from secondary causes such as stoves overturned by the blast wave.

The heat produced by an atomic explosion will set fire to easily ignitable materials such as dry grass and leaves, thin dark fabrics, and newspapers. The high-speed winds from the blast wave will put out many of these fires, but some (particularly dry rotted wood) will inevitably be left smoldering and may result fire outbreaks. To reduce this risk, whitewash the insides of window panes and remove flammable materials from locations where they may be exposed to heat radiation. These precautions will go a long way toward preventing fire outbreaks in areas where the nuclear blast is not severe. Fire extinguishers will also come in handy for putting out small fires before they become very destructive.

Dry forests and scrubland will also be prone to fire outbreaks. While it is less likely, very intense heat radiation could cause fires even in green vegetation, so it is best to avoid constructing a fallout shelter in bushy areas or forests.

Most of the fires at Hiroshima were started by secondary effects as opposed to heat radiation. An example would be a building that is destroyed when its furnace is on. You should ensure that you can protect yourself and your shelter from a fire outbreak on your own. Firefighting activities will be severely disrupted by a nuclear attack, with firefighters unable to reach fire outbreaks due to radioactive fallout and blast debris blocking the roads. Even if they can get to an area, broken water mains may mean that water pressure is inadequate for effective firefighting.

Most American basements can endure blast effects of up to 5 psi without severe injuries to their occupants. Fortification with stout posts and boards can increase protection well beyond that level. However, earth-covered shelters remain the best option, as they are safe from fire outbreaks as well as blast effects.

Even if a building does not catch fire, individuals inside could be killed by fiery-hot air, toxic smoke or carbon monoxide. Rubble-free fast burning fires produce high concentrations of carbon monoxide. If such a fire starts close to your shelter, the danger from carbon monoxide and carbon dioxide will remain high for about 90 minutes. The air intake for the ventilation system should not face, and should be as far as possible from, any building that could burn during a nuclear blast.

The firebombing of Dresden killed an estimated 135,000 people, many of them by carbon monoxide poisoning and the inhalation of smoke and hot gases. Those who fled their homes, even while the bombs were still dropping, had a better chance of survival than those who stayed indoors. This could apply to a nuclear attack as well, provided that the radioactive fallout is not severe. Even if it is, remaining in a shelter during an ongoing firestorm may give worse odds than leaving. However, if radiation meters show that radiation levels outside would be instantly fatal, you will need to remain where you are. Tightly shut all openings, which will help prevent carbon monoxide from entering your shelter and reaching a concentration that will lead to certain death. There is a chance that the fire outbreak will burn itself out before exhaled carbon dioxide builds up to fatal levels inside your sealed shelter. If you have built a separate earth-covered fallout shelter as opposed to using your basement, the heat should not become unbearable.

Food

Assuming you survive the blast and any subsequent firestorm, you will need food. For several reasons, it is vital that you prepare this in advance. The first of these is radioactive fallout. You will not be able to leave your shelter for several weeks after a nuclear attack, when the radiation will have decreased to a safe level. Continuous attacks could make it impossible to go outside for months. Adequate food must therefore be stored in your shelter (and/or close by) so that you can access it without exposure to the radioactive fallout.

Even if you could move around, food would probably be unavailable. Crops and livestock close to the blast will have been destroyed immediately. Radioactive fallout will then settle on other farmland, killing or contaminating plants and animals that survived the blast. Food will become very scarce and extremely expensive.

Humans need a certain minimum amount of food on a daily basis to stay healthy. Most people are used to eating more than this and may not understand that healthy adults can survive without any food for up to three weeks after an attack. (This does not apply to infants, children, the elderly, and the infirm, who may die from malnourishment within a week.)

It is very possible for most individuals to survive for months by eating just a few unprocessed staple foods. These are the foods with which you should stock your shelter. Having a good quantity of these foods on hand (as per the number of people staying in your shelter) will save you from the risk of leaving your shelter to search for food that will probably be unavailable anyway. You don't have to buy everything at once; all you have to do is stock up by buying small quantities on a regular basis for some time. For example, you could spend $50 to $100 on food for your shelter every month. If you do this consistently, within two years you should have enough food to sustain four people for over a year.

Buy foods that do not spoil easily, such as dried fruit. As long as they are stored in a dry place, these foods will remain safe for consumption for years, without losing their nutritional value. Canned meats, fruits and vegetables often last three years or more before they expire. Still, try to buy those that were manufactured very recently, i.e., within the past one to three months; this will extend the amount of time you can keep them in your shelter. Marmalade, chutney and jam are some good preserves to get. Baking powder, salt, sugar and flour can last for very long periods as long as they are kept dry. You should also stock your shelter with bottles of cooking oil and powdered milk. Get sacks of spelt, couscous, rice and pasta. Boiled chocolates and sweets are high in sugar and can provide quick energy when you are low on food supplies. Lentils and dried chick peas do well in long-term storage, have a high nutritional content, and are easily cooked just by boiling in water. You should also get spices and herbs to add flavor to your meals. If you can stock up on all these foods, you should be able to meet all your long-term nutritional needs.

Make sure to keep an eye on how quickly you are using up your food supply. If you have eaten half of it and are still not sure when you will be able to leave your shelter, you would be well advised to reduce your rations. It is better to be underfed until it is safe to come out than to eat well and run out of food while radiation levels are still high. When your supplies get very low, you may only have enough to eat once a week – but that is better than having nothing at all.

Even after radioactive fallout is no longer a concern, it is best to avoid surface foods for as long as possible, as they may contain harmful doses of radiation. For instance, a tasty-looking cow might have consumed grass or water contaminated by radioactive particles. If you eat the cow, you will ingest the radioactive particles as well. Especially avoid eating sick animals, as there is a very high likelihood that such animals are suffering from radiation poisoning.

Water

Water is one of the most basic requirements for life, but since it is generally available and easily accessible, most people take it for granted. Relatively few of us have experienced truly painful thirst, and while we may understand what it means to go without air for a minute, we cannot imagine going three days without water. In fact, water is considerably more important than food, as anyone who goes without it for a day or two will quickly realize. Survival in a fallout shelter will be impossible without an adequate supply of water.

For waste products to be effectively eliminated by the kidney, a person needs to drink enough water to produce at least 1 pint of urine every day. (When there is no shortage of water, most people produce about 2 pints of urine every day.) Apart from urine, we also lose water through excrement, exhaled breath and perspiration. Given cold weather and an uncrowded shelter, drinking 3 pints of water a day will be sufficient for weeks, especially when accompanied by a diet of small quantities of low-protein food. In hot weather, each person will require 4 to 5 quarts of water per day. Thus, 15 gallons of drinking water could last an individual two weeks. A family of four, planning for two months in a shelter, will therefore need 60 gallons per person, which comes to a total of 240 gallons. The water could be stored in the shelter or close by.

Using large containers to carry water to a shelter could be challenging, which makes it difficult to store enough water within a few weeks. It may be easier to transport water in polyethylene trash bags, which can also be used as waterproof liners for pillowcases or fabric bags. Avoid bags that are treated with chemicals to control odor or insects.

Many fallout shelters will not be big enough to store enough water to last one or two people for more than three weeks. In this case you can dig a pit for storing water very close to your shelter. Remove sharp rocks and roots from the wall of the pit, then fill it with containers or plastic bags full of water. Cover the top of the pit with a polythene bag to prevent rainwater from percolating downwards and contaminating your stored water. Fix the polythene to a circular wire hoop around the perimeter of the pit so that it will not fall into your water. Finally, cover the polythene with at least two feet of dirt.

For an easier option, just bury a tied bag of water in the pit and cover it with earth. However, the pressure from the loose earth may lead to leakage. You can reduce this by leaving a little airspace under a roofing of sticks or boards. Be careful when extracting the bag, as surrounding dirt may cave in and squeeze the bag when you remove the roof and earth covering.

If you have a very large container of water you obviously won't be able to lift it, and you will probably end up contaminating it if you dip a smaller container into it every time you fetch water. Siphoning the water out with a garden hose is therefore the best option, and with any luck you will be able to siphon it directly to your underground shelter. This way you won't need to leave the comfort of your shelter – and risk exposure to radioactive fallout

– when you need water. This will also reduce the risk of contaminating the water in the storage container.

Contamination with radioactive particles is certainly one concern, but you also have to worry about water-borne diseases. It is estimated that these diseases will actually kill more people than fallout following a nuclear attack. Furthermore, even nonpathogenic organisms can produce an unacceptable odor or taste in the water. You will therefore need a means of disinfecting your drinking water, especially if it has been stored in unclean containers or for a very long period of time. Airtight glass or thick plastic containers filled with sterile water should be safe for several years. Thin plastic containers such as old milk jugs are likely to develop leaks when stored for over two years.

Household bleach whose only ingredient is sodium hypochlorite, such as Clorox, can serve as a chlorine source for disinfecting water. Mix 1 teaspoon of bleach in 10 gallons of clear water, or 2 teaspoons in colored or muddy water. Wait at least 30 minutes before drinking to let the chlorine kill any microorganisms. If the water was properly disinfected you should perceive a slight chlorine odor. For small quantities of water, 2 drops of bleach will suffice for disinfection.

Wells will be a major source of water after a nuclear attack, but electric pumps may be rendered useless by the destruction of the electrical grid and electromagnetic pulse effects. It may therefore be necessary to use the old-fashioned method of tying a rope to an open container to fetch well water. The well water may be contaminated with radioactive particles and should therefore be filtered. As less than 2 percent of such particles are water soluble, filtration will be fairly effective in preventing casualties.

To filter well water, use nails to perforate the bottom of a 5-gallon bucket about a dozen times near the center. Add clean pebbles to the bucket to form a layer 1½ inches thick. If you don't have pebbles, you can use twigs or wire, such as from coat hangers. Cover the pebbles with a porous cloth like burlap or terrycloth. The cloth should form a circle about 3 inches larger in diameter than the bucket. Next you will need some soil. Take it from at least 4 inches below the surface, which will probably be contaminated with fallout particles. Try to find a good loam; sand will be too porous, and clay will not be porous enough. Pulverize the soil and then carefully press it over the cloth to create a layer 6 to 7 inches thick. Use a bath towel or the like to cover the soil so that it does not get eroded by the water. (The towel will also remove some particles itself.) Secure the towel with some small stones around the edges. Finally, place the filter you have created over a larger container, supported by sticks or metal rods. Pour contaminated water into the filter and allow it to drop into the larger container.

A second (and easier) option for filtration is the settling method. The drawback is that it takes longer. To use this method, fill a deep container, such as a bucket, up to 75 percent of its capacity with contaminated water. Find some clayey soil a minimum of 4 inches underground and mix it thoroughly with the water in the bucket, until it is entirely suspended. Then let the bucket sit for at least 6 hours. The clay will have settled to the bottom, taking most fallout particles along with it. You can then carefully siphon or scoop out the clear water. However, it is best to filter this water with the filtration method given above, especially if you plan to drink it.

When radiation levels have decreased enough that you can leave your shelter, take the opportunity to replenish your water supplies, especially if there is any danger of another nuclear attack. By this point any water you find should be radiologically safe, even without filtration, but remember that you will still need to disinfect it.

Meters for Radioactive Fallout

How can you tell when it is safe to leave your shelter? You cannot see, hear, taste, smell or feel radioactive fallout. Furthermore, since a heavy nuclear attack will destroy infrastructure and produce an electromagnetic pulse that interferes with radio waves, you probably won't be able to get information from the radio. The amount of time since the nuclear detonation will be one guide, but the best way to be certain that radioactivity has declined to a safe level is to use a radiation meter. Accurate, dependable radiation meters are available commercially, and you can easily find one online. It is also possible to make your own. If you know how to use one, it can tell you whether it is safe to leave your shelter at all, as well as how long you can spend outside. For example, it may be safe to go out for a few minutes to visit your water cache but still too radioactive to spend an hour foraging for other supplies.

Apart from knowing when it is safe to leave your shelter, you will also get some information about the shelter itself. Immediately after an attack, you should use the meter to find the part of your shelter with the lowest level of radioactivity. Remain in that area for at least several hours to get the best protection. By continuing to monitor the meter, you can calculate the radiation dose you are getting.

The radiation dose you receive determines whether you will suffer any adverse effects. Radiation exposure rate is measured in roentgen per hour (R/hr). Suppose your meter reads 2400 R/hr and you want to go outside for 15 seconds to empty your chamber pot. Dividing 2400 by 60 minutes gives 40 R/min. Since 15 seconds is ¼ minute, you divide this by 4 and get 10. Your exposure will therefore be 10 R, which should not produce any symptoms unless you receive it every day for more than week.

What if the exposure rate has fallen to just 30 R/hr and you would like to spend the whole day outside? Better not: 10 hours outdoors would represent an exposure of 300 R, enough to cause serious risk of death. The maximum exposure you should risk at one time is about 60 R, which will result in mild radiation poisoning symptoms. At 30 R/hr you might therefore be able to spend a couple of hours outside in search of water or food, but no more than that. After such an outing, you should limit your total radiation exposure over the next few days to less than 30 R.

Light

It is also important to think about lighting for your shelter. A pitch-dark shelter will be inconvenient and dangerous. People will already be very scared following a nuclear attack, and darkness will only add to the fear. When nobody can see anything and everyone is scared of what could happen next, people will tend to overreact to even the slightest sound. Some may become hysterical and violent. A dark shelter is a recipe for disaster, but adequate lighting will help maintain calm.

As noted above, the electricity will probably have gone off, so ordinary lighting won't work. Candles and flashlights will not help much, as they will be exhausted within a few days if you want to maintain 24-hour lighting in your shelter. They will last longer if you can synchronize the sleep/wake schedules of the occupants to allow for regular periods of darkness. For example, you could schedule 8 hours of sleep at night (say from 10 PM to 6 AM) and a 2-hour afternoon nap (maybe between 2 and 4). You will save about 10 hours of light this way. However, someone who wakes up in total darkness because he hears a noise or needs to relieve himself will be disoriented and may panic (or simply trip over another occupant on his way to the toilet), so this is not an ideal solution.

The best option is to combine a large battery with small, efficient battery-powered lights. You could use a car battery or a large dry cell battery and LED bulbs, for instance. Installing a high-capacity power inverter will provide a regular power supply for your shelter.

Shelter Sanitation and Preventive Medicine

Disposal of human waste will be one major challenge of shelter living, especially in public shelters holding over a thousand people. For family shelters, the simplest option is to use a 5-gallon bucket, wastebasket or paint can to collect both excrement and urine. Position it next to the exhaust vent and keep it tightly covered when not in use so that it will not attract flies.

When the container is full, dispose of it outside the shelter, still covered so as not to attract flies. Digging a latrine pit close to the shelter is also a good idea once radiation levels have declined enough to allow for outdoor bathroom breaks. (This will happen fairly soon; a minute or two of exposure will be safe even when radiation levels are still relatively high.) You can put up a blanket around the latrine to provide some level of privacy.

You should also be prepared to clean up and dispose of vomit. Vomiting is one symptom of radiation poisoning, and can also occur due to other illnesses or even as a result of anxiety.

And you must be prepared for the worst: Someone might die in your shelter, whether or not as a direct result of the nuclear attack. The sight and smell of a corpse in a confined space will be seriously disturbing, so you should stock your shelter with body bags in which you can store the deceased person until radiation levels are low enough for an outdoor burial. Perforate the bag so that it will not burst due to the buildup of gas produced by the decomposition of the body. As soon as the corpse starts to smell, it should be moved outside the shelter.

Consume only clean food and water. You can disinfect water by chlorination, as described above, or by boiling. To avoid contamination, do not dip containers into your main water source; instead, pour out some water into a smaller container that will hold enough for the day. Siphoning is an even better option.

Keep food in dustproof containers made of paper or plastic. You might want to hang the containers from the ceiling to protect them from moisture and bugs. If you smear some insecticide on the wire from which they're suspended, you won't have to worry about crawling insects. Make sure to keep your food preparation area clean and hygienic as well.

Self-Treatment and Medication

Unless you have a doctor in your family, or you're in a public shelter, you probably won't have access to one. Therefore you must be prepared to take care of injuries, burns and illnesses yourself. Toothache, childbirth, heat prostration, shock, broken bones, cuts from broken glass, infections and wounds are just a few of the conditions you may encounter. An excellent book on the subject is *Where There Is No Doctor*, which contains medical information far beyond the normal first aid treatments. Painkillers are one necessity, so get two boxes of extra-strength acetaminophen. As an anti-inflammatory, get two boxes of ibuprofen as well. Bandages for binding wounds will be required, and you should also get antiseptic cream, some sterilized needles and a strong, clean thread for sewing up wounds. A triangular bandage or sling should also be available. Cough drops and cough medicine are a good addition. Your first aid kit should include cotton wool, micropore tape, a bottle of sterile water, a roll of string (for numbing limbs that are being operated on), and iodine. Buy some good quality gas masks as well. Having all of these items in stock will allow you to treat most of the ailments it is possible to treat without specialized medical equipment.

Shelter Furnishings

In addition to bunks, your shelter should have chairs and a table. You will be more comfortable and productive if you can sit down at a table instead of spending the entire time lying in bed. Stock some interesting, easy-to-read books. If you have solar panels or a battery so you can charge your laptop and phone, it will be a good idea to load them with your favorite movies and music.

Also store in your shelter items that you will want to preserve, such as family heirlooms, rare books, gold and jewelry, birth certificates, diplomas, and photo albums. The amount of space in your shelter will place some limits on how much you can put inside, but insofar as possible you should try to make it into a place where you can spend several months without getting bored or idle.

Protective and Clothing Items

As already discussed, occupied shelters tend to be on the warm side, so you might not end up wearing heavy clothing. You should have some on hand anyway if there's any chance of cold weather where you live. Include duvets and space blankets along with the bed sheets so you can sleep warmly. Have a set of clothes that covers your neck and head to minimize heat loss. Long underwear and snow boots may be a good idea as well. A windbreaker is essential if you have to go outside in a strong, cold wind, and can also be used to control how much wind enters the shelter via the ventilation system. It can also provide some protection against beta burns (which occur when radioactive fallout settles on the skin).

If the shelter becomes too cold for you to be comfortable in the bedding and clothing you have, and you cannot light a fire, all occupants should stay close together to share body heat. Keep some insulating material between yourselves and the cold floor. If the floor is damp, put a plastic sheet below the insulating material. It's best to take these measures before you start to get cold. Once your blood vessels, especially those in your feet and hands, get constricted due to cold, it is difficult to restore them to normal dilation. The best thing to do when you are cold is to lie down and cover yourself up. Do not wave your hands or jump to stay warm; wind-chill caused by the resultant air movement will actually make you colder. If you become too warm and feel that you are about to start sweating, stand up or remove some clothes to avoid dampening your insulation with sweat. Smoking reduces blood flow to the feet and hands, so do not smoke if you are cold. You will also lose body heat more quickly after drinking an alcoholic beverage, because alcohol increases the flow of blood to the surface of your skin.

Protection

Looting is a significant risk in the aftermath of a nuclear attack. Career criminals may be expected to leap at the opportunity to enrich themselves by raiding houses. However, even ordinary people may be tempted to steal if they run out of supplies and get desperate. If guns are legal where you live, you should acquire any necessary permits and keep a firearm and some ammunition in a safe within your shelter. A gun will make it much easier to defend yourself if your life, water or food is threatened.

It is not necessarily a bad idea to share your supplies with those in need. But don't do so unless you can be sure that you will have enough to last you and your family. You do not want to risk giving away food and water only to find out that you have run out of supplies before help arrives. Consider yourself first. Once you are sure you will be fine, you can then begin to help others.

When War Is Imminent

If you have reason to believe that your locality is about to be attacked with nuclear weapons, the best thing to do is to evacuate. Immediately leave the high-risk area and travel to a low-risk area. In the event of hostilities between your country and another country, wherein the use of nuclear weapons is threatened, the area of lowest risk will be a third country. Moving to another country will be difficult and will involve leaving your home, your job and your kids' schools, but it will give you the best chance of staying alive and leading a normal life until the war is over. Make sure to leave at least a few days before the expiration of any ultimatum likely to trigger the use of nuclear weapons.

If you cannot or do not want to leave the country, you should assess the likelihood of a nuclear attack on your location. This will be highest if you are residing close to a strategic target such as an airport, military base, capital city, or other economically important city. The enemy will try to destroy such infrastructure to induce your country to surrender. If you live near one of these targets it will be best to relocate, ideally to a nearby rural area from which you can still commute to work. You will need to leave the house earlier, and you'll get home later, but at least you'll still have your job if the prospective war fizzles out. You can enroll your kids in the local school, and even if it isn't as good as the one they left, they'll be safe and alive – and that's obviously the most important thing.

If you absolutely must remain in a target area, follow the advice below to increase your chances of surviving an attack. It will also come in handy if there is a sudden attack and you have very little time to prepare.

Things to Do Prior to an Attack
When nuclear war seems likely, you must ensure that you can get information about an attack as soon as it is available. Many countries have developed early warning systems to alert their citizenry that a nuclear weapon has been launched against them. Usually, the system will be able to provide information on probable targets as well. Warning sirens are installed in cities and other strategic locations; when you hear the siren, you will

know that a missile is on its way. Learn what it sounds like and whether you will be able to hear it from your house.

If you won't be able to hear the warning directly from the siren, your next best bet is a radio. (You should unplug all other electrical devices to keep them from being destroyed by the electromagnetic pulse from the detonated nuclear weapon.) The media will relay the warning the instant it is sounded. When there is a threat of nuclear war, at least one person in your family should be listening to the radio (and/or television) at every single minute of the day. You can do this in shifts, but if there are children involved, make sure they understand the importance of informing you as soon as they hear any warning about a nuclear weapon heading towards your location. Once you get the warning, take cover immediately. Be prepared for multiple attacks, as it is very possible that more than one weapon will be deployed against a strategically important area.

During the Attack

When a nuclear device detonates, the first thing that will reach you is the flash, which travels at the speed of light. If you are outside, driving, or at a window when the detonation occurs, close your eyes as soon as you see the flash. Failure to do so could lead to permanent blindness. Then seek shelter immediately. If you are driving, park and look for shelter. You will have little chance of survival if you remain in the open too long. If you are away from home, your best bet is to find a hole or depression of some sort and quickly lie down in it. If you are near your shelter, get into it immediately. Remember to stay away from combustible/flammable materials.

Exposure to radiation will cause a large number of deaths. There are two types of radiation exposure: initial and residual. The initial radiation from the blast itself will travel only a short distance and will only last for a short period of time. The residual radiation comes from the radioactive fallout, which consists of debris and dust that are propelled into the atmosphere by the blast and then descend bearing a large quantity of fatal radiation. Fallout contaminates everything it comes in contact with, but you will be quite safe in a specially prepared shelter. You will be minimally protected in a normal house (which might not save you from radiation burns or even death), while you will have no protection whatsoever in an open environment. Your chances of survival increase substantially if you survive the blast and initial radiation, especially if you are already inside a shelter or are very close to one.

There are three major types of particles in radioactive fallout. These are alpha particles, beta particles and gamma rays. The alpha particles are the weakest and do not really pose any threat, as they survive for only a few inches before being absorbed in the atmosphere. (Inhaling or ingesting a substance that emits alpha particles could be fatal, however.) Beta particles are faster than alpha particles and can penetrate about 10 meters of air before being absorbed. They are only fatal after prolonged exposure.

Gamma rays are the deadliest of the particles. They travel in the atmosphere for almost a mile and can pass through virtually any type of shielding. Try to ensure that you are not exposed to gamma rays for more than five minutes. A well prepared shelter will protect you from about 99 percent of gamma rays. If you are in the open or in a rural area, look for a fallen log or cave you can crawl into. If there is none, lie down and dig yourself into a trench, piling dirt around you as you go.

If you are not in a prepared shelter, try to quickly reinforce whatever shelter you have found from the inside. Use anything you can find to cover the walls: wood, soil, concrete, books etc. If you are lying in a hole or trench try to create a roof with anything you can find around you, but do not leave to look for materials.

You will need to stay in your shelter for at least 200 hours, which works out to about 9 days. By then, all the fallout particles should have reached their half-life as a result of radioactive decay. However, you should continue to limit your exposure at this time. If your shelter is safe, stay there. If it is not, this will be your first opportunity to look for a better one. After 90 days only about 0.1 percent of the initial amount of radioactive fallout will be present in the atmosphere, and you will be much safer.

Figure out now how your food will be shared among the people in your shelter and how long it will last. If you have enough food and water, you should plan to stay in your prepared shelter for at least 90 days, until radiation exposure is no longer a threat. Otherwise, ration the food to last as long as possible, hopefully at least fourteen days, which is when you can start to consider going out briefly to search for food. Make sure to return to the shelter as quickly as possible. Since most of the fallout remains on the surface, it will be safe to eat most food and fruits after you remove the outside covering.

If you have to go out when the radiation level is still high, wear as much clothing as possible. A long sleeve shirt, goggles, gloves and a hat will reduce your exposure. Constantly shake your clothes, and wash them later to get rid of particles that have settled on them. If you do get radiation burns, treat them by washing blisters and broken or charred skin with cold water. Don't break the blisters or cover the burns, even if a large part of the skin is affected.

Minimum Pre-Crisis Preparation

If you are limited by budget or other factors but still want to improve your chances of surviving a nuclear attack, you are probably wondering what the most important items to acquire are. The most important, of course, is a shelter capable of protecting you from radioactive fallout. Choose an area with hard soil and dig with a shovel and a bow saw. Rainproof your shelter with 4-mil polyethylene film.

You need ventilation for your shelter, so get an air pump (or several, depending on the size of the shelter). Store enough water for everybody who will be staying in the shelter. Keep a hose handy so that you can use it to siphon water from the reservoir. You might also want to make a water filter and get some sodium hypochlorite bleach bottle handy for disinfecting water and utensils. Buy a radiation meter and also learn how to use it.

You will need to eat to stay strong and alive, so food is also vital. Buy foodstuffs with years of shelf life, preferably ready to eat or simple to cook, and stockpile them in your shelter. Draw up a plan for rationing food in case your supplies run low before it is safe to go outside.

Sanitation supplies will also be necessary. Line the inside of a 5-gallon bucket with a heavy plastic bag and vent it with a hose. This will serve as toilet. Stock up on toilet paper and tampons for female members of your household. Fly bait and mosquito netting will help to reduce insect problems.

If anyone in your family needs a particular medication, make sure you have it in sufficient quantity in the shelter. You should also have a first aid kit containing a tube of antibiotic ointment so that you can effectively respond to any medical emergencies that might come up.

If you cannot afford to install a proper lighting system, buy enough small-wicked candles to last for at least 14 nights. You might also want to get a lamp and a flashlight with extra batteries.

A transistor radio (again with extra batteries) might also be useful, if radio services happen not to go off in your area. They are very inexpensive, so this is a case where it is better to have one and not need it than need one and not have it.

Aside from the above, include any items that you personally consider essential – whatever you cannot ordinarily do without. Put these items in your shelter so that they will be there whenever the time comes to hunker down.

Conclusion

A nuclear war anywhere in the world is expected to lead to a very high level of loss in terms of property and human lives. Proper preparation will increase your probability of surviving such a war. The biggest danger from a nuclear attack is the blast; the next biggest is the radioactive fallout; and fires and carbon monoxide poisoning are the third-ranking danger for unprepared individuals. To survive a nuclear attack, it is crucial to get as much information as possible on these dangers and to undertake adequate preparatory measures against each of them.

This book has listed and explained a number of items that will be very important in the event of a nuclear attack. Having all of these items in place and getting to them before radioactive fallout gets to you means that you will probably survive. A personal underground shelter outside your house, covered with about three feet of earth and stocked with all the necessary items, is your best bet. If this is infeasible, reinforce your basement and stock it with supplies. If the initial blast and fire do not destroy your house, you should be safe. If you have made no preparations at all when a nuclear attack comes, go to your basement or to a public shelter. Staying in your house will expose you to high risk and make survival unlikely.

The minimum preparations for a nuclear attack include shelter, an air pump for ventilation, water, a radiation meter, food, sanitation and medical supplies, lighting, and a radio. Do not expect life to go back to normal immediately after the war. The government will require some time to repair the damage to the infrastructure and restore normalcy. School and work will probably be suspended indefinitely, but more importantly food may not be readily available for quite some time. Try to stockpile enough food to last well beyond the 90 days you will need to spend in your shelter. Having enough to eat in the weeks and months after the war ends will ensure that you do not have to pay profiteers' prices or travel long distances to buy food.

Further Reading

How to Survive the Next Nuclear Attack, https://www.nationallibertyalliance.org/files/survival/how_to_survive_the_next_nuclear_attack.pdf

Kearny C.H., Nuclear War Survival Skills, 1987 edition, http://www.madisoncountyema.com/nwss.pdf

Canada Emergency Measures Organization, 11 Steps to Survival, http://www.jumpjet.info/Emergency-Preparedness/Disaster-Mitigation/Civil/11_Steps_to_Nuclear_Survival.pdf

Also by Macallister Anderson

Printed in Great Britain
by Amazon